TRICK EYES

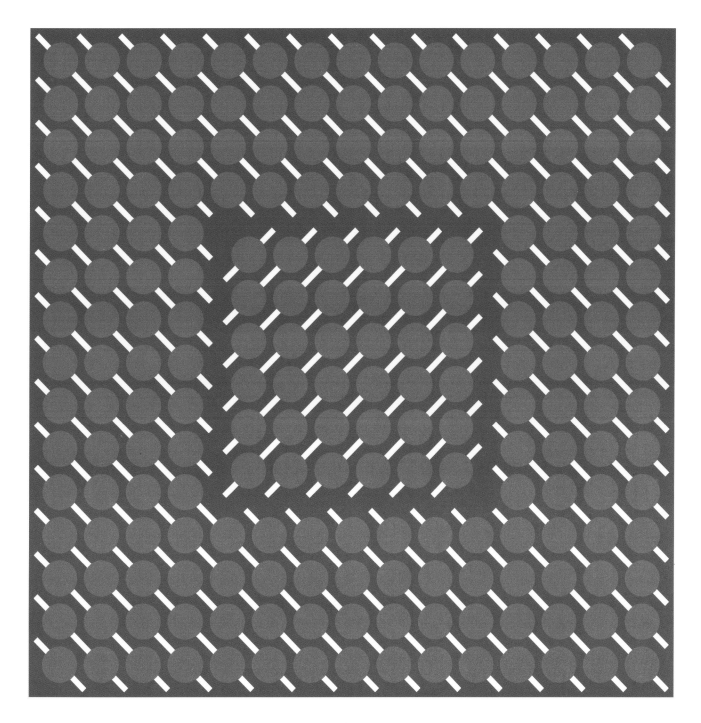

Akiyoshi Kitaoka

BARNES & NOBLE

NEW YORK

Title page artwork:

Packed Cherries   **motion illusion**

The inset appears to move. When the image is moved up
and down, the inset appears to move right and left.

"TRICK EYES" written and supervised by Akiyoshi Kitaoka
© Akiyoshi Kitaoka 2002. © KANZEN.
All rights reserved.

"TRICK EYES 2" written and supervised by Akiyoshi Kitaoka
© Akiyoshi Kitaoka 2003. © KANZEN.
All rights reserved.

Original Japanese books published by Kanzen, Tokyo.

First U.S. edition published by Barnes & Noble Publishing, Inc.,
2005

This English language combined edition is published by arrangement with Kanzen Inc., Tokyo through Tuttle-Mori Agency, Inc.,
Tokyo.

2005 Barnes & Noble Publishing

ISBN-13: 978-0-7607-6698-9
ISBN-10: 0-7607-6698-3

Printed in China

3 5 7 9 10 8 6 4

CONTENTS

Part I: Introduction to Visual Illusion

Everyone Can See Illusions!

Visual Illusions

Welcome to the Illusion World

Part II: Exploring the Visual Illusion World

Everyone Can See!

Visual Illusions

Welcome to the Illusion World

Part I: Introduction to Visual Illusion

Candy

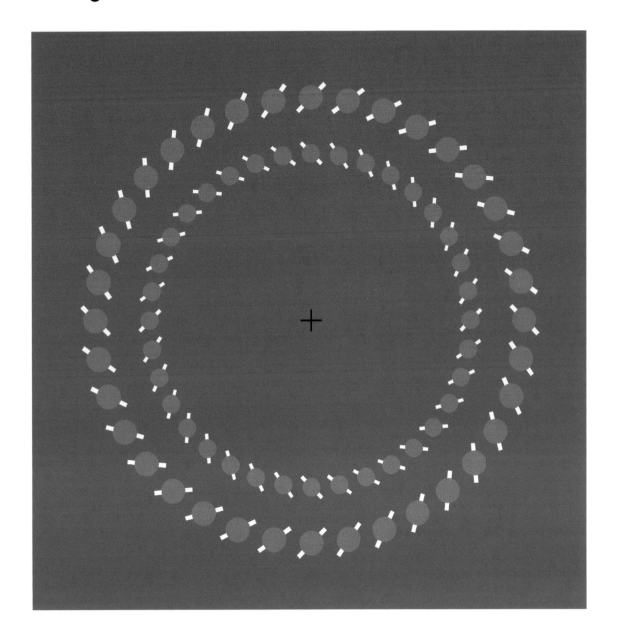

When observers approach or move away from the image, keeping their gazes at the cross, the two rings appear to rotate in directions opposite to each other.

Everyone can see illusions!

Draw the power hidden in your brain by seeing visual illusion!

The brain is activated by visual illusion

When we see something, we are usually sure of correct perception. But we happen to see objects in the wrong manner. Such misperception is called "visual illusion." Everyone can see visual illusions to a greater or lesser degree, probably because the visual system of eyes and the brain does not adopt sequentially controlled computation but does jumping processes or "tricks."

It is suggested that visual illusions should activate the brain. Visual illusion surprises us even if we know it well. This is due to the discrepancy between the perceived image of an object and the knowledge of its physical property. Surprise increases the level of arousal, activating the brain. Figure 1 shows a neural system that plays a role on arousal called the reticular activating system or the ascending activating system.

Needless to say, visual illusions are amusing. In this regard, a visual illusion has an aesthetic aspect because there is actually an unnoticed "principle" that the greater the illusion magnitude, the more beautiful the image. Moreover, visual illusions trigger curiosity, which is the mother of science. It is therefore suggested that seeing a visual illusion should activate the brain to raise your mind to art and science.

Figure 1. A schematic presentation of the reticular activating system or the ascending activating system. The reticular formation penetrates the midbrain, pons, and the medulla oblongata, receives inputs from sensory tracts, and activates a large part of the regions of the cerebral cortex.

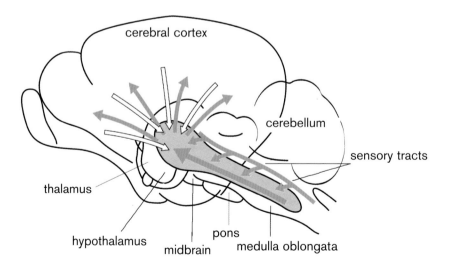

*This drawing shows an animal's brain, which is functionally identical to the human brain.

How to enjoy visual illusion

The best way to enjoy visual illusion is to see many images of high quality illusions. This book includes a variety of images of the highest (I believe) quality. However, it is generally difficult for many people to get such books of high quality because most of them are academic ones that are not sold every-where. To solve this problem, one can access the Internet and find illusion pages. Key words are "illusion" or "visual illusion." Please also try to access my homepage entitled "Akiyoshi's illusion pages" (*http://www.ritsumei.ac.jp/~akitaoka/index-e.html*), which contains a tremendous number of original illusion designs created by me. "Illusion forum" given by NTT Communication Science Laboratories *(http://www.brl.ntt.co.jp/IllusionForum/menu-e.html)* is amusing as well as educational. I think the oldest illusion webpage, which had started in 1995 before the Internet spread, is "The open space for Visual Illusion" produced by the Tokyo Metropolitan University *(http://psywww.human.metro-u.ac.jp/sakusi/index_e.htm)*.

If you would like to expand your enjoyment of visual illusions, I recommend that you try to create illusion designs by yourself. I will teach you how to design visual illusion in the next section.

How to design visual illusion

As mentioned before, the greater the illusion magnitude, the more beautiful the image. Probably many researchers of visual illusion implicitly know this "principle," but most of them have never mentioned it because there is no full evidence to prove the principle. That is, the question of whether visual illusion renders aesthetic sensation or beautiful images enhance visual illusion has not been answered yet.

According to this principle, everyone who learns how to design visual illusion can be an artist because illusion designs give aesthetic sensation without exception. Let's be an artist!

It is not so difficult to produce illusion images. First, you need a PC and a printer. Secondly, a draw program is necessary, but you do not need to buy an expensive one like Adobe Illustrator. A program attached to a word processor is enough because most illusion designs are made up of lines, circles, or squares.

You may want to use an ink-jet printer rather than a laser printer because prints from a laser printer are sometimes uneven. Because marketed printers nowadays go beyond the resolution, color, and printing speed that we need for illusion designs, any ink-jet printer is okay. Are you ready? Let's start to create illusion designs. What did you say? You cannot do so because you cannot discover any new illusion by yourself? Don't worry.

Please try to produce your original work by combining known elemental illusions. Here I will show an example.

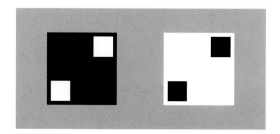

Figure 2. Elemental images of the checkered illusion. They consist of only squares but appear to tilt when seen from far away.

Figure 2 is an elemental image of the "checkered" illusion I proposed in 1998. This figure consists of only squares. You can produce an illusion work, for example, by merely repeating the elemental images like Figure 3.

Figure 3. An illusion work named "Dice." Vertical edges appear to tilt counterclockwise while horizontal edges appear to tilt clockwise.

After you finish a work, it is recommended to immediately give it a name, e.g. "Dice," because it is rather difficult to remember the work afterward if it has no name. If "Dice" and its mirror image are combined, you obtain a new image that appears to bulge out (Figure 4).

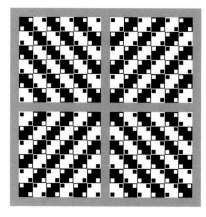

Figure 4. An arrangement to give a convex or a "bulging outward" appearance, where the apparent tilts are placed so that whole edges appear to curve outward.

Moreover, you can also modify it to produce a work including motion illusion (Figure 5).

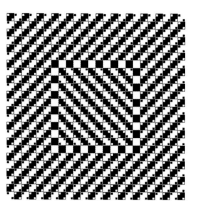

Figure 5. An illusion work called "A Trampoline," in which the inset appears to move. Because the figural characteristics of motion illusion are often the same as those of geometrical illusion, motion illusion is sometimes found by chance when creating images of geometrical illusion.

Furthermore, you can color images as long as the relative lightness between adjacent regions is not changed (Figure 6).

It is thus easy to produce illusion designs. Let's start to be an artist today!

Figure 6. Coloring a monochromatic illusion design does not disturb the illusion as long as the relative lightness between adjacent regions is not changed.

How to enjoy science with visual illusion

A visual illusion is one of the most popular educational materials for scientific experiments. The most significant advantage is that both materials and results are visible. It is also advantageous that everyone can see a visual illusion if the illusion magnitude is large enough. Moreover, observers can enjoy the process of producing illusion designs throughout easy experiments. Furthermore, a visual illusion is an "error" in visual processing, which dodges the belief that science should not make any mistakes.

This indicates that everyone can enjoy science with visual illusions without difficulty.

Actually, science is amusing. My belief is that it is not science if it is not amusing. It is thus my greatest pleasure that children can understand the fun of science by playing with visual illusions. Of course, adults also have the right to have fun with visual illusions and science.

Let's go to the world of illusion.

An Approaching Asteroid

motion illusion, color illusion

When you move the image up and down, the inset appears to move up and down. When you rotate the image, the inset appears to rotate with delay. If you quickly approach the image, the inset appears to loom with delay. In addition, for some observers, the apparent depth of the inset is different from that of the surface of the surround. This phenomenon is called chromostereopsis.

Tiger

When you approach or move away from the image keeping your gaze at the center, the ring appears to rotate. The areas other than the ring may appear to rotate in the opposite direction.

Maccha

The rows of gray dots appear to move horizontally. In addition, the rows appear to tilt alternately though they are actually parallel.

(*Maccha* means "powdered tea.")

A Snake

Concentric rings appear to form a spiral.

The Autumn Color Swamp

The inner square area appears to move. When the image projected into the eyes is moved vertically, the inset appears to move horizontally. On the other hand, when the image is moved horizontally, the inset appears to move vertically. In addition, edges that are actually vertical or horizontal appear to tilt, and the apparent tilts in the inset are opposite to those in the surround.

Nuts

The inset appears to move. When the image projected into the eyes is moved vertically, the inset appears to move horizontally. On the other hand, when the image is moved horizontally, the inset appears to move vertically. Many observers will see this illusion without any action because eyes move involuntarily.

Ferryboats

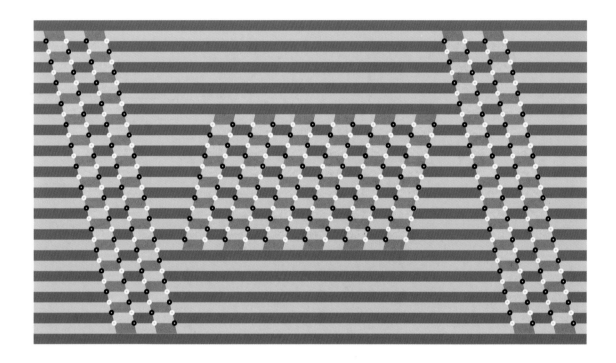

The inner six bars appear to slide horizontally. This illusion is generated by moving the image up and down. In addition, some parts of horizontal edges appear to tilt.

Makudonarudo

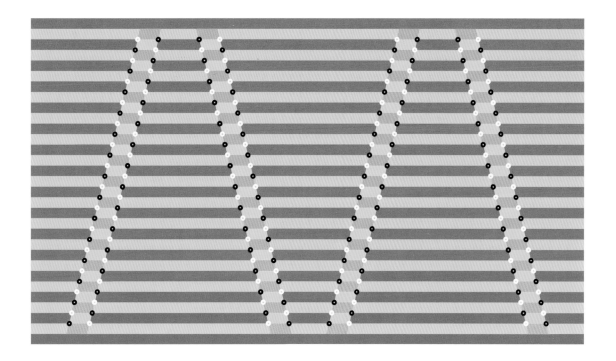

The yellow bars appear to move horizontally. This illusion is caused by moving the image up and down. In addition, some parts of horizontal edges appear to tilt.

(*Makudonarudo* is the pronunciation of McDonald's™ in Japanese.)

The Floating Heart

color illusion, motion illusion

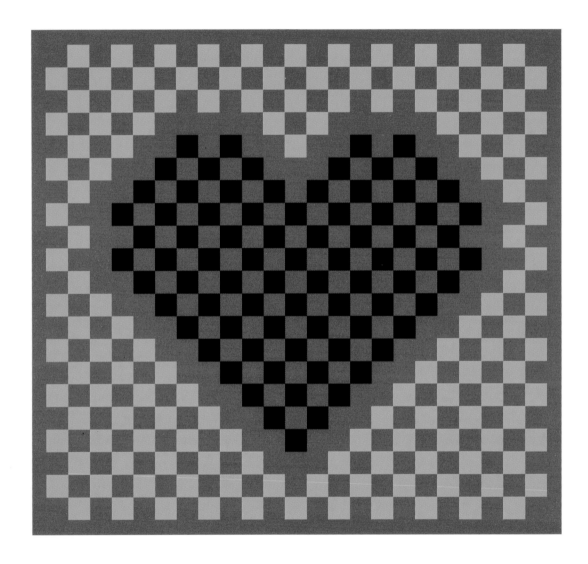

For more than half of our viewers, the black heart appears to be in front of the surface of the surround. For some observers, the former appears to be behind the latter. This phenomenon is called chromostereopsis (as described on p. 6). Moreover, the black heart appears to move.

Bavarian Cream

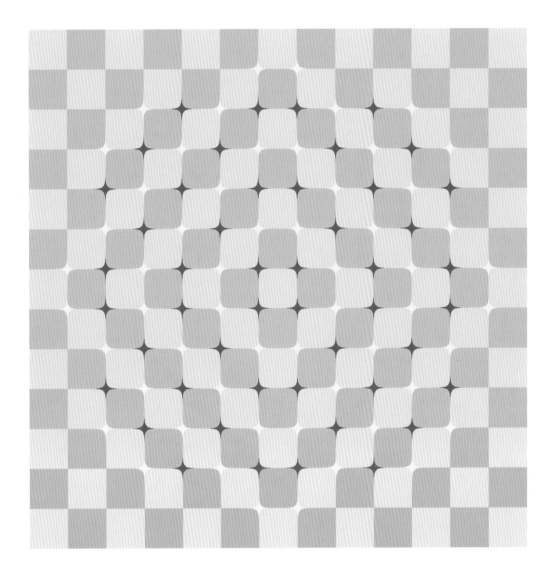

The checkerboard pattern actually consists of squares, but the image appears to bulge out due to geometrical illusion. Slight motion illusion gives an impression like Bavarian cream or pudding.

Primrose's Field

The image appears to wave. This illusion is so strong that involuntary eye movement alone can generate this effect.

Green Spirals

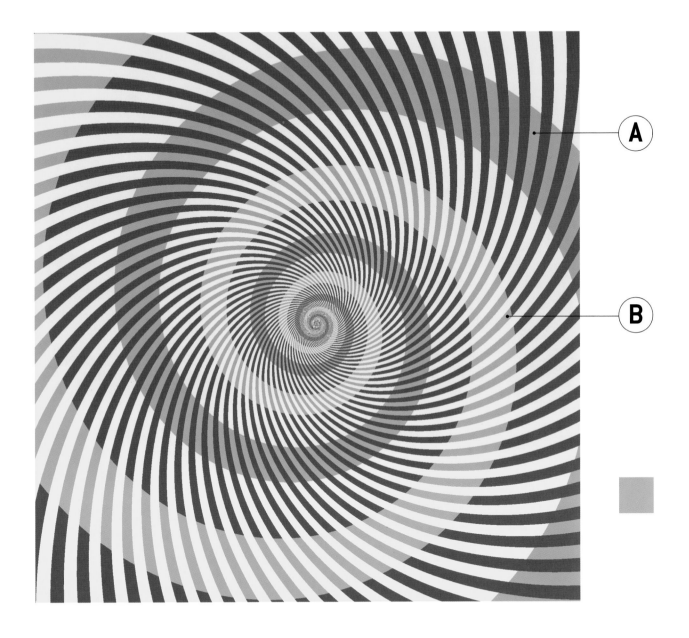

It appears that there are blue-green (A) and yellow-green (B) spirals, but they are quite identical in color! In addition, when observers approach or move away from the image keeping their gazes at the center, the grating appears to rotate.

Kids of Seals

Concentric arrays of dots appear to form spirals that go to the center by rotating counterclockwise.

The Neural Network

spiral illusion, rotating illusion

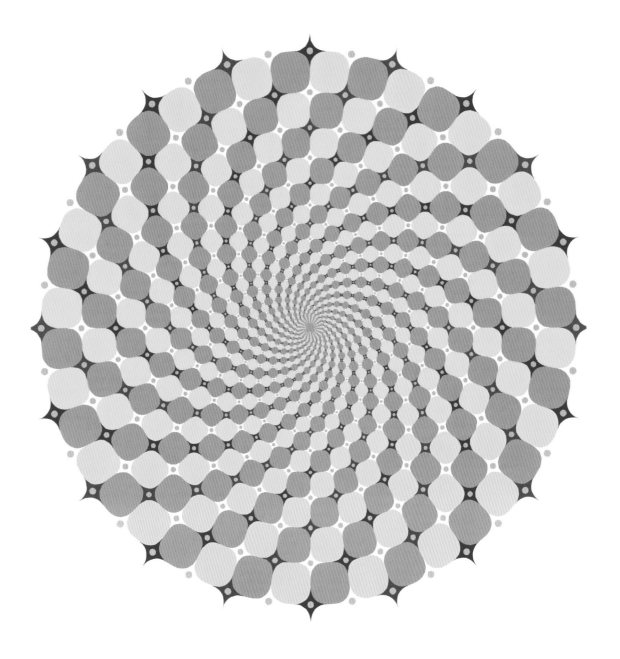

Although star-shaped "neurons" are aligned on concentric circles, they appear to form spirals that go to the center by rotating clockwise. Moreover, when observers approach or move away from the image keeping their gazes at the center, the image appears to rotate counterclockwise or clockwise.

Barber Spirals

The gray lines are actually concentric circles but appear to form spirals that go to the center by rotating clockwise.

Primrose's Spirals

spiral illusion, rotating illusion

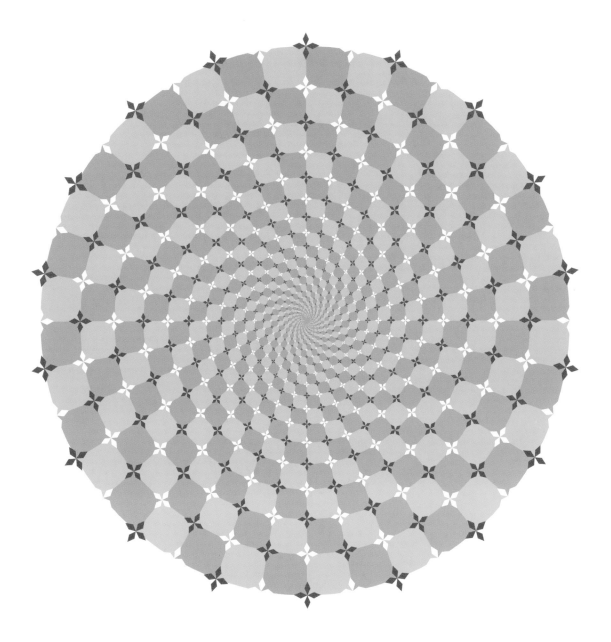

"Flowers of primrose" actually form concentric circles but appear to be aligned in a spiral fashion that goes to the center by rotating clockwise.

Primrose's Circulation

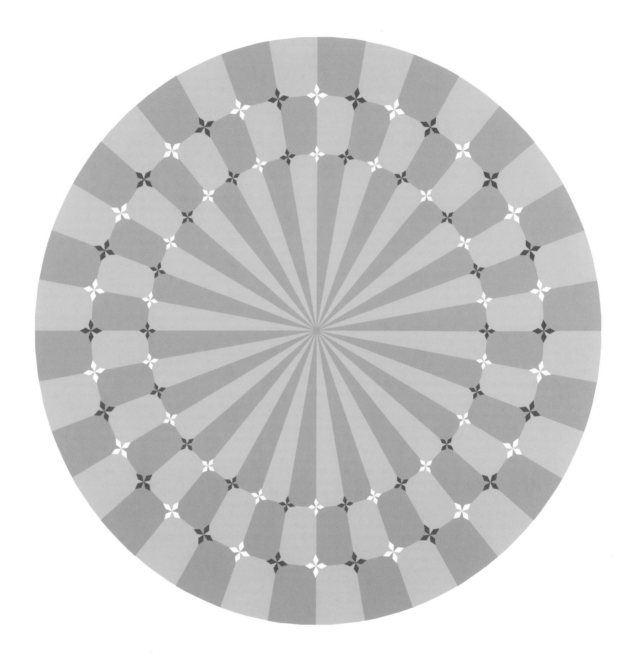

When observers rotate the image keeping their gazes at the center, the gap between the two rings appears to increase or decrease. It is puzzling because such motion perception does not change the physical size of the gap.

Koinobori

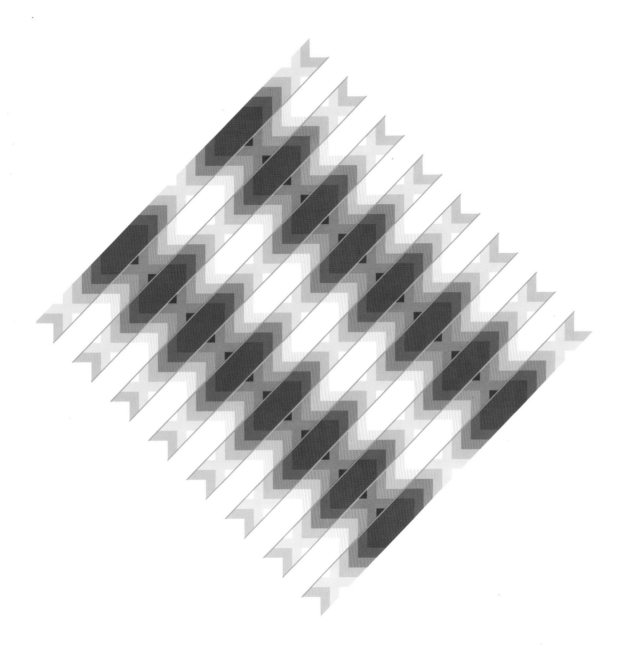

Oblique yellowish-green lines are actually straight and parallel to each other but appear to curve. This illusion is caused by both the Zöllner Illusion *(p. 61)* and the illusion of shifted gradations I proposed in 1998.

(*Koinobori* are carp-shaped streamers, which are raised above the roofs of houses to celebrate the growth of young boys in Japan on May 5.)

Autumn Color

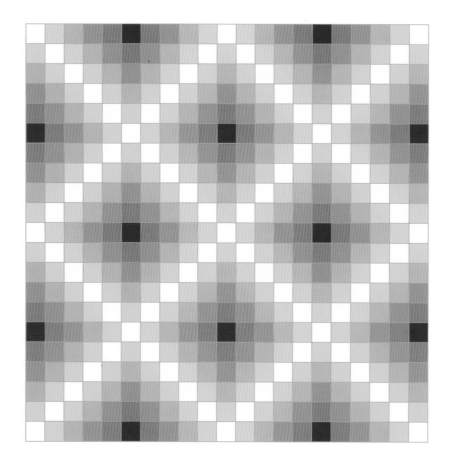

The verticals and horizontals appear to curve.

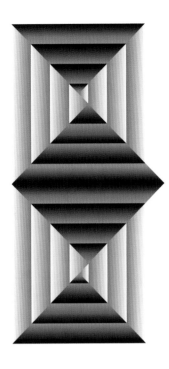

An Hourglass

perceptual transparency

There appear two square
spirals that are translucent.

A Lens

geometrical illusion

The image consists of only
squares but its middle area
appears to bulge out.

Welcome to the illusion world

1. History of the study of visual illusion

The psychological study of visual illusion started in the middle of the nineteenth century, about one hundred fifty years ago. Most images of geometrical illusions were discovered in the latter half of the nineteenth century and in the beginning of the twentieth century, followed by extensive study of visual illusion. However, the activity of the study gradually decreased in the latter half of the twentieth century. This tendency did not indicate that the quality of the study of visual illusion decreased, but that the number of researchers tackling visual illusion decreased. This decrease partly depended on the misunderstanding that the study of visual illusion should have been exhausted.

The study of visual illusion, however, has entered a new period (or the third period) characterized by the term "IT revolution." "IT" usually indicates "information technology," but I here mean the "illusion" technology, which includes PCs and printers that have come to be ubiquitous. This IT is much smaller in extent than the original IT but is revolutionary enough for the study of visual illusion.

The media to produce illusion was paper in the study of visual illusion's first period (the "discovery" period from the middle of the nineteenth century to the beginning of the twentieth century) and second period (the "development" period over the twentieth century). Researchers used to draw or paint images with pen and ink on pieces of paper. That is, pens, ink, and paper were the tools for the study of visual illusion. These were inexpensive and ubiquitous, so researchers who were not well funded were able to

start studies of visual illusion without difficulty. This condition largely contributed to the development of the study of visual illusion.

There was a problem, however. It was necessary for researchers to draw images skillfully. For this reason, researchers and drawers were often separate persons. To find some hint for the study of visual illusion, researchers had to keep observing images from the beginning of drawing. Such a chance thus tended to be missed. Moreover, line drawing was preferred to painting because it was difficult to paint images completely with ink, especially with gray ink or color ink. Therefore, most of the images of visual illusion were line drawings before the third period.

The spread of PCs and printers has solved this problem. For example, it took much time and much skill to get a square filled with gray with pen and ink, but it is now very easy to do so with a PC and a printer. Using a drawing software we only draw a square with a "rectangle tool" filled with gray "property." Most skills of drawers are not necessary. Moreover, we can freely change every property after finishing an image. Furthermore, CRT or LCD monitors give images of lower resolution like 1024 x 768 pixels, but a printer prints images of much higher resolution.

I thus imagine that the beginning of the twenty-first century is the third period or the "second discovery" period of the study of visual illusion. Indeed, publication of new illusions has been increasing.

2. Classification of visual illusions

This book classifies visual illusions into geometrical illusion, spiral illusion, motion illusion, rotating illusion, lightness illusion, color illusion, etc., but this classification is not so standard. For example, a spiral illusion is a kind of geometrical illusion, and a rotating illusion is a kind of motion illusion. I think classification of visual illusions has not been established yet.

Geometrical illusion, which is the most popular class of visual illusions, is often classified into size illusion like the Müller-Lyer Illusion, orientation illusion like the Zöllner Illusion, and position illusion like the Poggendorff Illusion. But this classification has not been widely accepted, either.

Motion illusion, which is featured in this book, belongs to a new class of visual illusion that has recently been developing. In this book, motion illusion, or the "anomalous motion illusion" in several studies, refers to an illusion in which part or all of a stationary image appears to move. The Ouchi Illusion was the only motion illusion in the twentieth century, but the number of motion illusions has abruptly been increasing in the twenty-first century. Thus the classification of motion illusion is necessary in the near future.

3. A catalogue of visual illusions

It may be difficult for many people to obtain academic books that explain visual illusions. I will demonstrate typical or famous illusions in the following two pages.

frequently used for the education of psychology because the illusion magnitude is much larger than that of other size illusions.

Typical Visual Illusions

Müller-Lyer Illusion

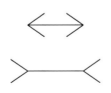

When arrowheads are attached inward to both ends of a line segment such as in the upper image, the segment appears to be slightly shorter than it is. On the other hand, when arrowheads are attached outward to both ends of a line segment as in the lower image, the segment appears to be considerably longer than it is. In this figure, the upper line segment appears to be shorter than the lower one though they are identical in length. This illusion is

Zöllner Illusion

Parallel lines appear to tilt in the directions that acute angles formed with obliquely crossing lines expand. In this figure, the five horizontal lines are actually parallel, but the uppermost one appears to tilt counterclockwise, the second one appears to tilt clockwise, and so on.

Poggendorff Illusion

The two oblique line segments are actually aligned, but the top-right one appears to be slightly higher in position than it is.

Ponzo Illusion

The two line segments are actually the same length, but the one nearer to the apex of the inverted "V" appears to be longer than the other.

Jastrow Illusion

The two curving images are actually the same size, but the inner one appears to be larger than the outer one.

Oppel-Kundt Illusion

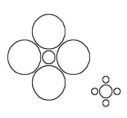

The second bar counted from the right is physically placed just in the middle of both ends, but appears to shift rightward.

Ebbinghaus Illusion

When a circle is surrounded by larger circles, its size appears to be smaller than it is. On the other hand, when a circle is surrounded by smaller circles, its size appears to be larger than it is. This illusion is also called the Titchener Illusion.

Fick Illusion

The length of the vertical is the same as that of the horizontal, but the former appears to be longer than the latter. This illusion is also called the Vertical-Horizontal Illusion.

Hering Illusion

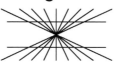

The two parallel lines appear to curve and to bulge out.

Shepard Illusion

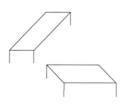

The two parallelograms are identical in shape and size but do not appear so. (R. N. Shepard. *Mind Sights: Original Visual Illusions, Ambiguities, and Other Anomalies, with a Commentary on the Play of Mind in Perception and Art*. New York: Freeman, 1990.)

Gravity-lens Illusion

The four dots are placed at the apices of a virtual parallelogram, but the position of each appears to shift toward the nearest one of the black circles. (S. Naito and J. B. Cole. "The Gravity Lens Illusion and Its Mathematical Model." *Contributions to Mathematical Psychology, Psychometrics and Methodology*. Eds. G. H. Fischer and D. Laming. New York: Springer-Verlag, 1994.)

Café Wall Illusion

When rows of black and white squares are shifted with a quarter phase to each other and gray lines are placed between the borders, the lines appear to tilt though they are parallel. The uppermost line appears to tilt counterclockwise, the second one clockwise, and so on.

Hermann Grid Illusion

Illusory black spots appear at the crosses of white streaks. This effect is weak at the gazing point.

Scintillating Grid Illusion

Illusory black spots appear to sparkle in white circles placed on the crosses of gray streaks. Like the Hermann Grid Illusion, the effect is weak at the gazing point. (M. Schrauf, B. Lingelbach, and E. R. Wist. "The Scintillating Grid Illusion." *Vision Research* 37 (1997): 1033-1038.)

Ouchi Illusion

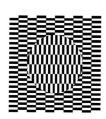

When a vertically elongated checkerboard pattern is combined with a horizontally elongated checkerboard pattern, the inset appears to move. (L. Spillmann, F. Heitger, and S. Schuller. "Apparent Displacement and Phase Unlocking in Checkerboard Patterns." Paper presented at the ninth European Conference on Visual Perception, Bad Nauheim, 1986.)

Kanizsa Figure

Although there are merely four "pacmen," observers feel as if a white square is placed in front of four black circles. This figure is a typical pattern of visual completion.

Neon Color Spreading (neon lightness spreading in this case)

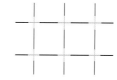

When the crosses of a black grating are replaced with gray crosses, white patches of round or diamond shape appear to cover or hover on the crosses.

Logvinenko Illusion

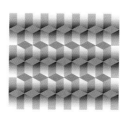

There appear dark-gray diamonds and light-gray ones, but they are identical in lightness. This effect is so strong that many readers may possibly miss what I meant. (A. D. Logvinenko. "Lightness Induction Revisited." *Perception* 28 (1999): 803-816.)

White Illusion

When a gray grating is placed on the black phase of a black-and-white grating, it appears to be lighter than it is. On the other hand, when a gray grating is placed on the white phase of a black-and-white grating, it appears to be darker than it is.

Subjective Color

Illusory tints appear to run in the direction orthogonal to the inducing black-and-white grating.

Makkurokurosuke

op effect, motion illusion

The surround appears to scintillate or oscillate. I think the former is the Scintillating Grid Illusion *(p. 112)* and the latter depends on the difference in apparent speeds between the inset and the surround.

(The title of *Makkurokurosuke*, carbon creatures or black fairies that are thought to live in a deserted house, is taken from one of the popular Japanese animations, *Tonari no totoro*.)

The Metro

This is a stereogram. Try to fuse the two blue dots with cross-fusing or uncross-fusing *(p. 67)*, then the second and fourth lines made up of yellow and black squares will appear to tilt in depth. Moreover, green broken lines sometimes appear to shift their depths, which is called the Wallpaper Illusion.

Scintillation by Binocular Rivalry

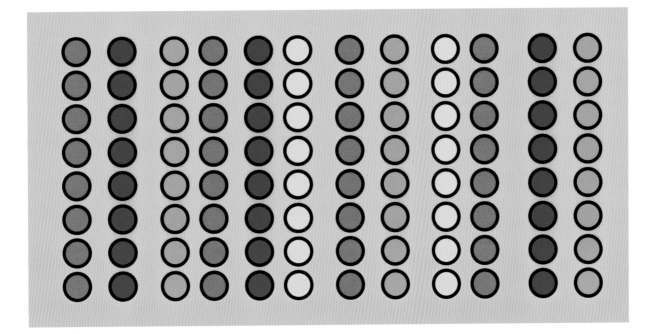

This is a stereogram. Try to fuse the adjacent circles with cross-fusing or uncross-fusing *(p. 67)*, then each of the vertical rows appears to be on one of several surfaces within a three-dimensional image. When red circles are, for example, given to the right eye and green ones to the left eye, scintillation or alternation between red and green is seen. This phenomenon is called binocular rivalry.

Floating Dice

This is a stereogram. Try to fuse the two blue dots with cross-fusing or uncross-fusing *(p. 67)*, then there will appear squares in front of the whole image or square windows through which another surface is visible behind the image. Moreover, these squares or windows appear to move. In addition, these patterns consist of vertical or horizontal edges, but they appear to tilt.

A River in Autumn
stereogram, motion illusion, geometrical illusion

This is a stereogram. Try to fuse the two red stars shown below the image with cross-fusing or uncross-fusing *(p. 67)*, then there appears a transparent river. Moreover, leaves of autumn color (red or yellow stars) appear to move. In addition, edges other than red or yellow stars are actually vertical or horizontal but appear to tilt.

Scintillation of Red

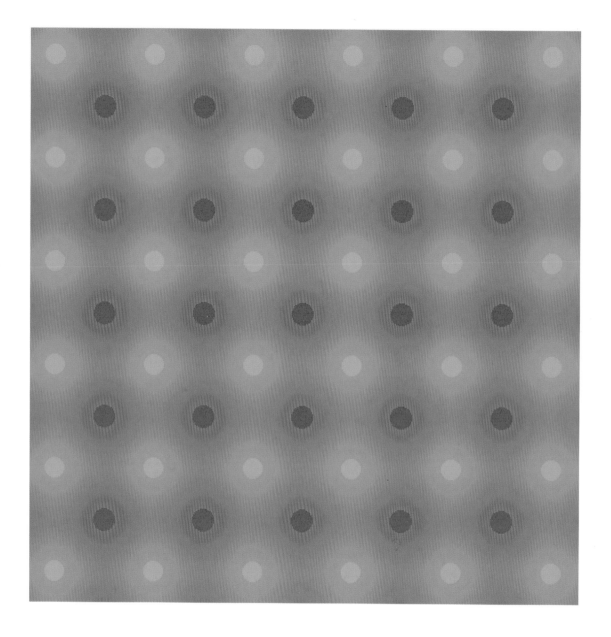

Red circles appear to scintillate when rapid eye movements (saccades) occur.
I speculate that this effect is generated by a delay of visual processing of red as
compared with blue. This speculation challenges the accepted thought that blue
takes a longer processing time than red does.

Red Swirls

The painted red is homogeneous over the image, but the red in the center or the red seen in the peripheral vision appears to be magenta (red-purple).

A Flower Shop

The red surrounded by yellow circles appears to be orange while the red surrounded by blue circles appears to be magenta (red-purple), though they are identical.

Exploration

The blue background appears to expand, while the red ring appears to contract. Moreover, it appears as if the ring were slowly moving away. Furthermore, when observers approach or move away from the image keeping their gazes at the center, the ring appears to rotate. In addition, when observers approach the image keeping their gazes at the center, the redness of the ring is enhanced.

Expanding Cushions

peripheral drift illusion, geometrical illusion

Each cushion appears to expand. In addition, vertical or horizontal gray lines in each cushion appear to curve inward.

Sitting Up All Night

spiral illusion, peripheral drift illusion

Red concentric circles appear to form spirals. The right circle appears to rotate clockwise, while the left rotates counterclockwise.

The Sun

Vertical or horizontal edges appear to tilt and the image appears to bulge out.
It sometimes gives a slightly moving impression.

The Sun in Summer

Rows of dots appear to wave, though they are actually aligned on radials.

Red Threads

Red threads are all straight but appear to curve. In addition, the background appears to move occasionally.

When a Ship Leaves Port

geometrical illusion

Oblique lines are all straight and parallel to each other but appear to curve.

Author's Note: I am from Kochi in the Shikoku island, with which ferries used to connect the main island (called Honshu) of Japan before the islands were connected by a series of giant bridges *(Seto-ohashi)*. Ferries left port drawing "farewell tapes."

Nautilus Pompilus

A white "spiral mist" can be seen. Actually the modification of color or lightness is given only to the purple-red parts, while the white parts of radials are homogeneous, but the mist appears to be continual and to be in front of the radials. This effect is called the Visual Phantom Illusion.

Precious Metals

Vertical rows appear to move up and down. Moreover, "black noise" appears to sparkle on white parts.

Cubism

The inset appears to slide slowly. While "Cubism" is the name of a movement of art in the beginning of the twentieth century, I merely would like to show that images of cubes can yield motion illusion.

Blocks

Rows of color blocks appear to move. Specifically, the first (red), third (blue), and fifth (yellow) rows from the left appear to move in the bottom-left direction, while the rest appear to move in the top-right direction.

Kaminari-san

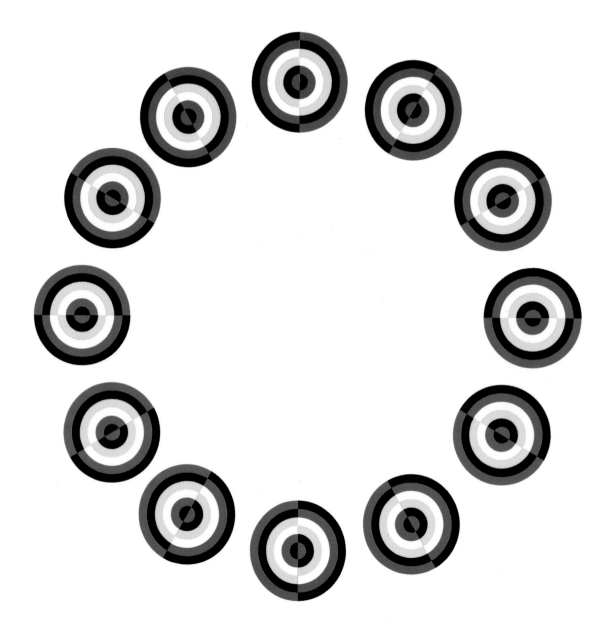

The ring of Kaminari-san's *taiko* (drums) appears to rotate clockwise.

(*Kaminari-san* refers to an imaginary god of thunder who sheds the light and sound of thunder.)

Pinecones

The central piece of "Pinecones" appears to move. When observers move the image up and down, the inset appears to move right and left.

The Rainbow Wave

The image occasionally appears to wave. The elemental motion illusion is called the Pinna-Brelstaff Illusion.

This explanation is acceptable enough for experts but may be difficult for non-experts. Imagine a rotating barber pole, the surface of which is painted with red, blue, and white stripes. The pole is rotating with the axis being the vertical, but stripes appear to ascend rather than rotate. This phenomenon is called the Barber-Pole Illusion, which partly shares a common explanation with the present rotating illusion.

This acceptable explanation, however, is flawed by an illusion design shown in Figure 4, in which the two rings appear to rotate in directions opposite to each other when observers approach or move away from the image keeping their gazes at the center. This characteristic may appear to be the same as that in Figure 1, but the difference exists in that the directions of apparent rotation are opposite to those in Figure 1, though the orientations of line segments are the same as those in Figure 1. Specifically, when you approach the image, the outer ring appears to

rotate clockwise in Figure 4 while it appears to rotate counterclockwise in Figure 1.

To solve this problem, Ikuya Murakami (NTT Communication Science Laboratories), one of my collaborators, proposed a band-pass filtering model. Band-pass filtering is similar to a filtering used in photo-retouching software to blur, sharpen, or reverse images. In this model, band-pass filtering of a particular parameter does not change the directions of apparent rotation in Figures 1 and 4 or the orientation of line segments in Figure 1, but it does reverse the orientation of line segments in Figure 4. These results are shown in Figures 5 and 6. In short, this model shows that Figure 4 is attributable to Figure 1 because they have a similar mechanism in terms of processing in the brain, which may be acceptable for experts.

The science of visual illusion, as well as illusion design, is steadily advancing.

Figure 5.
The bandpass-filtered image of Figure 1. The orientation of line segments and the rotating illusion are both retained.

Figure 6.
The bandpass-filtered image of Figure 4. Although the orientation of line segments is reversed, the direction of apparent rotation is retained. This result suggests that Figure 4 be attributable to Figure 1 because they are processed similarly in the brain.

Author Profile

Akiyoshi Kitaoka is Associate Professor of
Psychology at the Department of Psychology,
College of Letters, Ritsumeikan University, Kyoto,
Japan. He received his B.Sc. from the Department
of Biology, University of Tsukuba, Tsukuba, Japan, in
1984, and received his Ph.D. (Doctor of Education)
from the Institute of Psychology, University of
Tsukuba, in 1991. He has extensively studied visual
illusion including geometrical illusion, lightness
illusions, color illusions, motion illusion, and so on.
Before he started to investigate visual illusions,
he had studied animal psychology, especially
burrowing behavior in rats at the University of
Tsukuba, and neurophysiology of the monkey
inferotemporal cortex in the Tokyo Metropolitan
Institute for Neuroscience. He has rigorously been
exhibiting his illusion designs on his home page
(www.ritsumei.ac.jp/~akitaoka/index-e.html)
since 2002.